Reagan

by Iain Gray

LangSyne
PUBLISHING
WRITING *to* REMEMBER

Lang**Syne**

PUBLISHING

WRITING *to* REMEMBER

Office 5, Vineyard Business Centre,
Pathhead, Midlothian EH37 5XP
Tel: 01875 321 203 Fax: 01875 321 233
E-mail: info@lang-syne.co.uk
www.langsyneshop.co.uk

Design by Dorothy Meikle
Printed by Hay Nisbet Press, Glasgow
© Lang Syne Publishers Ltd 2009

ISBN 978-1-85217-309-8

Reagan

MOTTO:
The hills forever.

CREST:
A griffin.

NAME variations include:
Ó Ríagáin (Gaelic)
O'Reagan
O'Regan
Regan

Chapter one:

Origins of Irish surnames

**According to an old saying, there are two types of Irish –
those who actually are Irish and those who wish they were.**

This sentiment is only one example of the allure that the
high romance and drama of the proud nation's history holds
for thousands of people scattered across the world today.

It's a sad fact, however, that the vast majority of Irish
surnames are found far beyond Irish shores, rather than on
the Emerald Isle itself.

The population stood at around eight million souls in
1841, but today it stands at fewer than six million.

This is mainly a tragic consequence of the potato
famine, also known as the Great Hunger, which devastated
Ireland between 1845 and 1849.

The Irish peasantry had become almost wholly reliant
for basic sustenance on the potato, first introduced from the
Americas in the seventeenth century.

When the crop was hit by a blight, at least 800,000
people starved to death while an estimated two million
others were forced to seek a new life far from their native
shores   particularly in America, Canada, and Australia.

The effects of the potato blight continued until about
1851, by which time a firm pattern of emigration had
become established.

Ireland's loss, however, was to the gain of the countries in which the immigrants settled, contributing enormously, as their descendants do today, to the well being of the nations in which their forefathers settled.

But those who were forced through dire circumstance to establish a new life in foreign parts never forgot their roots, or the proud heritage and traditions of the land that gave them birth.

Nor do their descendants.

It is a heritage that is inextricably bound up in the colourful variety of Irish names themselves – and the origin and history of these names forms an integral part of the vibrant drama that is the nation's history, one of both glorious fortune and tragic misfortune.

This history is well documented, and one of the most important and fascinating of the earliest sources are *The Annals of the Four Masters*, compiled between 1632 and 1636 by four friars at the Franciscan Monastery in County Donegal.

Compiled from earlier sources, and purporting to go back to the Biblical Deluge, much of the material takes in the mythological origins and history of Ireland and the Irish.

This includes tales of successive waves of invaders and settlers such as the Fomorians, the Partholonians, the Nemedians, the Fir Bolgs, the Tuatha De Danann, and the Laigain.

Of particular interest are the *Milesian Genealogies*,

because the majority of Irish clans today claim a descent from either Heremon, Ir, or Heber – three of the sons of Milesius, a king of what is now modern day Spain.

These sons invaded Ireland in the second millennium B.C, apparently in fulfilment of a mysterious prophecy received by their father.

This Milesian lineage is said to have ruled Ireland for nearly 3,000 years, until the island came under the sway of England's King Henry II in 1171 following what is known as the Cambro-Norman invasion.

This is an important date not only in Irish history in general, but for the effect the invasion subsequently had for Irish surnames.

'Cambro' comes from the Welsh, and 'Cambro-Norman' describes those Welsh knights of Norman origin who invaded Ireland.

But they were invaders who stayed, inter-marrying with the native Irish population and founding their own proud dynasties that bore Cambro-Norman names such as Archer, Barbour, Brannagh, Fitzgerald, Fitzgibbon, Fleming, Joyce, Plunkett, and Walsh – to name only a few.

These 'Cambro-Norman' surnames that still flourish throughout the world today form one of the three main categories in which Irish names can be placed – those of Gaelic-Irish, Cambro-Norman, and Anglo-Irish.

Previous to the Cambro-Norman invasion of the twelfth century, and throughout the earlier invasions and settlement of those wild bands of sea rovers known as the Vikings in the eighth and ninth centuries, the population of the island was relatively small, and it was normal for a person to be identified through the use of only a forename.

But as population gradually increased and there were many more people with the same forename, surnames were adopted to distinguish one person, or one community, from another.

Individuals identified themselves with their own particular tribe, or 'tuath', and this tribe – that also became known as a clann, or clan – took its name from some distinguished ancestor who had founded the clan.

The Gaelic-Irish form of the name Kelly, for example, is Ó Ceallaigh, or O'Kelly, indicating descent from an original 'Ceallaigh', with the 'O' denoting 'grandson of.' The name was later anglicised to Kelly.

The prefix 'Mac' or 'Mc', meanwhile, as with the clans of the Scottish Highlands, denotes 'son of.'

Although the Irish clans had much in common with their Scottish counterparts, one important difference lies in what are known as 'septs', or branches, of the clan.

Septs of Scottish clans were groups who often bore an entirely different name from the clan name but were under the clan's protection.

In Ireland, septs were groups that shared the same name and who could be found scattered throughout the four provinces of Ulster, Leinster, Munster, and Connacht.

The 'golden age' of the Gaelic-Irish clans, infused as their veins were with the blood of Celts, pre-dates the Viking invasions of the eighth and ninth centuries and the Norman invasion of the twelfth century, and the sacred heart of the country was the Hill of Tara, near the River Boyne, in County Meath.

Known in Gaelic as 'Teamhar na Rí', or Hill of Kings, it was the royal seat of the 'Ard Rí Éireann', or High King of Ireland, to whom the petty kings, or chieftains, from the island's provinces were ultimately subordinate.

It was on the Hill of Tara, beside a stone pillar known as the Irish 'Lia Fáil', or Stone of Destiny, that the High Kings were inaugurated and, according to legend, this stone would emit a piercing screech that could be heard all over Ireland when touched by the hand of the rightful king.

The Hill of Tara is today one of the island's main tourist attractions.

Opposition to English rule over Ireland, established in the wake of the Cambro-Norman invasion, broke out frequently and the harsh solution adopted by the powerful forces of the Crown was to forcibly evict the native Irish from their lands.

These lands were then granted to Protestant colonists, or 'planters', from Britain.

Many of these colonists, ironically, came from Scotland and were the descendants of the original 'Scotti', or 'Scots', who gave their name to Scotland after migrating there in the fifth century A.D., from the north of Ireland.

Colonisation entailed harsh penal laws being imposed on the majority of the native Irish population, stripping them practically of all of their rights.

The Crown's main bastion in Ireland was Dublin and its environs, known as the Pale, and it was the dispossessed peasantry who lived outside this Pale, desperately striving to eke out a meagre living.

It was this that gave rise to the modern-day expression of someone or something being 'beyond the pale'.

Attempts were made to stamp out all aspects of the ancient Gaelic-Irish culture, to the extent that even to bear a Gaelic-Irish name was to invite discrimination.

This is why many Gaelic-Irish names were anglicised with, for example, and noted above, Ó Ceallaigh, or O'Kelly, being anglicised to Kelly.

Succeeding centuries have seen strong revivals of Gaelic-Irish consciousness, however, and this has led to many families reverting back to the original form of their name, while the language itself is frequently found on the fluent tongues of an estimated 90,000 to 145,000 of the island's population.

Ireland's turbulent history of religious and political strife is one that lasted well into the twentieth century, a landmark century that saw the partition of the island into the twenty-six counties of the independent Republic of

Ireland, or Eire, and the six counties of Northern Ireland, or Ulster.

Dublin, originally founded by Vikings, is now a vibrant and truly cosmopolitan city while the proud city of Belfast is one of the jewels in the crown of Ulster.

It was Saint Patrick who first brought the light of Christianity to Ireland in the fifth century A.D.

Interpretations of this Christian message have varied over the centuries, often leading to bitter sectarian conflict – but the many intricately sculpted Celtic Crosses found all over the island are symbolic of a unity that crosses the sectarian divide.

It is an image that fuses the 'old gods' of the Celts with Christianity.

All the signs from the early years of this new millennium indicate that sectarian strife may soon become a thing of the past – with the Irish and their many kinsfolk across the world, be they Protestant or Catholic, finding common purpose in the rich tapestry of their shared heritage.

Chapter two:

High Kings and Vikings

**With roots firmly embedded in the ancient soil of
Ireland, the Reagans of today can claim a proud descent
from some of the island's greatest warrior kings.**

One indication of their royal origins can be found in the
Gaelic-Irish form of the name itself, Ó Ríagáin, which stems
from 'Rí', signifying 'King'.

The Reagans were to be found scattered throughout
the Emerald Isle from the earliest times, including in
what is now East Cork, near the present day town of
Fermoy.

The Reagan presence in East Cork is remembered to this
day in the town names of Coolyregan and Ballyregan, while
they were also to be found at Ballinaclogh, in the province
of Connacht.

But it was in the modern day county of Meath, and in the
former kingdom of Thomond in the northern reaches of the
province of Munster, that the Reagans stamped a particular
mark on the pages of Ireland's turbulent story.

The Reagans of Meath traced their descent from
Riaghan, a grandson of Flann Da Congal, who in turn was
in a direct line of descent from Heremon, one of the island's
earliest monarchs.

Heremon was one of the sons of Milesius, a king of

what is now modern day Spain, and who had planned to invade Ireland in fulfilment of a mysterious Druidic prophecy.

He died before he could launch his invasion across the sea to Ireland, but eight sons who included Amergin, Hebor, Ir, and Heremon undertook the task.

Five sons, including Ir, were killed in battle against the Tuatha-De-Danann shortly after battling their way from the shoreline to the soil of Ireland.

This was soil, however, that Ir's offspring and the offspring of his brothers Heber and Heremon were destined to hold for centuries as warrior kings.

According to the Milesian genealogies, Heremon and Heber began to rule the land they had conquered from about 1699 B.C. – with Heremon later killing Amergin and Heber in quarrels over territory.

Along with the O'Hares, Connollys, and Kellys, the Reagans of Meath made up what were known as the princely and celebrated Four Tribes of Tara, with Tara the sacred site of the enthronement of the Ard Rí, or High King, of Ireland.

The four tribes, whose territories were divided up into south and north Brega, were part of the great clan confederation that formed the southern Hy Niall, or Uí Neill, and who traced a descent from Fiacha, a son of the legendary Niall Noíghiallach, better known to posterity as the great warrior king Niall of the Nine Hostages.

The dramatic life and times of this ancestor of the Reagans are steeped in stirring Celtic myth and legend.

The youngest son of Eochaidh Mugmedon, king of Connacht, his mother died in childbirth and he was brought up by his evil stepmother Mongfhinn who was determined that he should die.

She accordingly abandoned him naked on the Hill of Tara, but he was found by a wandering bard who took him back to his father.

One legend is that Mongfhinn sent Niall and his four brothers – Brian, Fiachra, Ailill, and Fergus – to a renowned prophet who was also a blacksmith to determine which of them would succeed their father as Ard Rí.

The blacksmith, known as Sitchin, set the lads a task by deliberately setting fire to his forge.

Niall's brothers ran in and came out carrying the spearheads, fuel, hammers, and barrels of beer that they had rescued, but Niall staggered out clutching the heavy anvil so vital to the blacksmith's trade.

By this deed, Sitchin prophesied that Niall would be the one who would take on the glorious mantle of kingship.

Another prophetic incident occurred one day while Niall and his brothers were engaged in the hunt.

Thirsty from their efforts, they encountered an ugly old woman who offered them water – but only in return for a kiss.

Three of the lads, no doubt repelled by her green teeth

and scaly skin, refused. Fiachra pecked her lightly on the cheek and, by this act, she prophesied that he would one day reign at Tara – but only briefly.

The bold Niall, however, kissed her fully on the lips. The hag then demanded that he should now have full sexual intercourse with her and, undaunted, he did so.

Through this action she was suddenly transformed into a stunningly beautiful young woman known as Flaithius, or Royalty, who predicted that he would become the greatest High King of Ireland.

Mongfhinn later tried to poison him, but accidentally took the deadly potion herself and died.

This legend relates to what was known as the Festival of Mongfhinn, or Feis na Samhan (the Feast of Samhain), because it was on the evening of October 31, on Samhain's Eve, that the poisoning incident is said to have taken place.

It was believed for centuries in Ireland that, on Samhain Eve, Mongfhinn's warped and wicked spirit would roam the land in hungry search of children's souls.

The Festival, or Feast, of Samhain, is today better known as Halloween.

Niall became Ard Rí in 379 A.D. and embarked on the series of military campaigns and other daring adventures that would subsequently earn him the title of Niall of the Nine Hostages.

The nine countries and territories into which he raided

and took hostages for ransom were the Irish provinces of Munster, Leinster, Connacht, and Ulster, Britain, and the territories of the Saxons, Morini, Picts, and Dalriads.

Niall's most famous hostage was a young lad known as Succat, son of Calpernius, a Romano-Briton who lived in the area of present day Milford Haven, on the Welsh coast.

Later known as Patricius, or Patrick, he became renowned as Ireland's patron saint, St. Patrick, responsible for bringing the light of Christianity to the island in the early years of the fifth century A.D.

Raiding in Gaul, in the area of Boulogne-sur-mer in present day France, Niall was ambushed and killed by one of his treacherous subjects in 405 A.D.

It was through their descent from Niall's son, Fiacha, that the southern Hy Niall clans such as the Reagans of Meath were also known as Cenel Fhiachaigh, or Fiachach.

The Reagan hold on their Meath territory was often precarious, particularly in the face of foreign invasion.

It was in the closing years of the eighth century A.D. that the sinister longboats of the Vikings first appeared off Irish shores, and the monastery of St. Patrick's Island, near Skerries in present day Co. Dublin, was looted and burned to the ground.

Raids continued along the coastline until they made their first forays inland in 836 A.D., while a year later a Viking fleet of 60 vessels sailed into the River Boyne.

An indication of the terror they brought can be found in

a contemporary account of their depredations and desecrations.

It lamented how 'the pagans desecrated the sanctuaries of God, and poured out the blood of saints upon the altar, laid waste the house of our hope, trampled on the bodies of saints in the temple of God, like dung in the street.'

By 841 A.D. the Vikings, or Ostmen as they were also known, had established a number of strongholds on the island, but their raids began to ease off before returning with a terrifying and bloody vengeance in about 914 A.D.

They met with a determined resistance from the native Irish, most notably in the form of the forces of the powerful confederation of clans of the southern Uí Neill.

The Irish suffered a resounding defeat at the battle of Dublin in 919 A.D., and it was not until just over thirty years later that the raids gradually came to an end.

By this time the Vikings had established permanent settlements in Ireland, particularly in Dublin and other coastal areas such as present day Waterford, Wexford, Carlingford, and Strangford – indeed the names of the latter four stem from the Old Norse language of the Scandinavians.

But warfare with the native Irish such as the Reagans was still endemic, and it is recorded that in the early eleventh century Matgamain Ó Ríagáin, the Reagan king of Brega at the time, inflicted a memorable defeat on Amlaoibh, a son of Sitric, the Viking king of Dublin.

Chapter three:

Rebel cause

The Reagans of the kingdom of Thomond, in common with the proud clan of O'Brien, traced a descent from the famed Race of Cas, also known as the DalgCais, or Dalcassians.

The Dalcassians were named from the legendary Cormac Cas, the early to mid-third century chieftain of the province of Munster who was renowned for his remarkable courage, strength, and dexterity.

This ancestor of the Reagans inflicted a celebrated defeat on the men of the province of Leinster in a battle fought near present day Wexford, but was killed in battle in 254 A.D. at Dun-tri-Liag, or the Fort of the Stone Slabs, known today as Duntrileague, in Co. Limerick.

His deathblow, according to the ancient annals, came from the spear of the Leinster king known rather colourfully as Eochy of the Red Eyebrows.

But it was at the side of a descendant of Cormac Cas that the Reagans of Thomond, in common with their Meath namesakes, also resisted the Viking invader.

This was no less a figure than Brian Bóruma mac Cénnetig, a younger son of Cennetig, king of Thomond, and who was born about 926 A.D.

It was largely through his inspired leadership that Viking

power was diminished, although not completely eliminated.

He was able to achieve this by managing to rally a number of other chieftains to his cause.

With his battle-hardened warriors known as the Dalcassian knights at his side, Boru had by 1002 A.D. achieved the prize of the High Kingship of Ireland – but there were still rival chieftains, and not least the Vikings, to deal with.

But, resenting Boru's High Kingship, a number of chieftains found common cause with the Ostmen, and the two sides met in final and bloody confrontation at the battle of Clontarf, four miles north of Dublin, on Good Friday 1014.

Boru proved victorious, but the annals speak of great slaughter on the day, with the dead piled high on the field of battle.

Among the many dead were Brian Boru's three sons, while he was killed by a party of fleeing Vikings, but not before felling most of them with his great two-handed sword.

It is through Riagan – a grandson of Boru's brother Cineadh – that the Reagans of Thomond trace their descent from the great warrior king.

The Ua Ríagáin, or Reagans, were honoured in 2003 with official membership of today's Clan of the DalgCais, whose patron is the O'Brien Chief of the Name, the O'Brien of Thomond, also Lord Inchiquin.

Less than 200 years after Boru's victory over the Vikings at the battle of Clontarf, the island found itself at the mercy of a new wave of ruthless invaders.

These ambitious and battle-hardened Norman barons and adventurers who had settled in Wales in the aftermath of the Norman Conquest of England in 1066, descended on Ireland in 1169 and swiftly amassed territory.

By 1171 England's Henry II had claimed Ireland as his own, receiving the reluctant submission and homage of many of the Irish chieftains – and one contemporary account of these tragic times was penned by a Maurice O'Regan.

English dominion over Ireland was ratified through the Treaty of Windsor of 1175, under the terms of which the Reagans, for example, were only allowed to rule territory unoccupied by the Normans in the role of a vassal of the king.

It only proved to be a recipe for disaster as the island was frequently torn apart by bloody insurrection and rebellion against the increasingly harsh policies of the English Crown.

At the root of the rebellion was the Crown's policy of settling, or 'planting' loyal Protestants on Irish land, a policy that had started during the reign of Henry VIII and continued under successive monarchs.

In the grim centuries following the original Norman invasion and the subsequent influx of new waves of English and Scottish settlers, the Reagans of Meath found themselves inexorably pushed westwards into an area of what is now Queen's County, or County Laois.

By the sixteenth century the Reagans of East Cork had been driven into what is now the area of West Cork, while the Reagans of Thomond had to struggle to retain their ancient rights and privileges in a territory that is today encompassed by parts of Co. Limerick.

What is perceived by many as the final death knell of the ancient Gaelic Order of clans such as the Reagans was sounded in 1688 in what is known as Cogadh an Dá Rí, or The War of the Two Kings.

Also known as the Williamite War in Ireland, it was sparked off when the Stuart monarch James II, under threat from powerful factions who feared a return to the dominance of Roman Catholicism under his rule, fled into exile in France.

The Protestant William of Orange and his wife Mary were invited to take up the thrones of Scotland, Ireland, and England – but James had significant Catholic support in Ireland.

His supporters were known as Jacobites, and among them was Sir Tiege MacShane O'Regan, the last of the chiefly line of the name in West Cork, and who was born in 1629.

Following the arrival in England of William and Mary from Holland, Richard Talbot, 1st Earl of Tyrconnell and

James's Lord Deputy in Ireland, assembled an army loyal to the Stuart cause.

The aim was to garrison and fortify the island in the name of James and quell any resistance – and James later knighted Tiege O'Regan for his part in defending militarily strategic forts in his role as governor of Sligo.

Londonderry, or Derry, proved loyal to the cause of William of Orange, or William III as he had become, and managed to hold out against a siege that was not lifted until July 28, 1689.

James, with the support of troops and money supplied by Louis XIV of France, had landed at Kinsale in March of 1689 and joined forces with his Irish supporters.

A series of military encounters followed, culminating in James's defeat by an army commanded by William at the battle of the Boyne on July 12, 1690.

James fled again into French exile, never to return, while another significant Jacobite defeat occurred in July of 1691 at the battle of Aughrim – with about half their army killed on the field, wounded, or taken prisoner.

The Williamite forces besieged Limerick and the Jacobites were forced into surrender in September of 1691.

A peace treaty known as the Treaty of Limerick followed, under which those Jacobites willing to swear an oath of loyalty to William were allowed to remain in their native land.

Those reluctant to do so, including many native Irish

such as Sir Tiege O'Regan and his kinsfolk, chose foreign exile – their ancient homelands lost to them forever.

A further flight overseas occurred following an abortive rebellion in 1798.

Reagans were also among the many thousands of Irish who were forced to seek a new life far from their native land during the famine known as The Great Hunger, caused by a failure of the potato crop between 1845 and 1849.

But Ireland's loss of sons and daughters such as the Reagans was to the gain of those equally proud nations in which they settled.

Chapter four:
On the world stage

Generations of bearers of the name of Reagan, in all its variety of spellings, have achieved distinction in a colourful range of pursuits.

Arguably the most famous bearer of the name of Reagan, at least in contemporary times, was the actor and politician **Ronald Reagan**, who had the distinction of serving two successive terms as the 40th President of the United States.

Born in 1911 in Illinois of Irish-Scots ancestry, Reagan worked as a young man on radio stations in Iowa and later as an announcer for Chicago Cubs baseball games.

It was while travelling through California with the Cubs in 1937 that he decided to take a screen test – a move that was destined to radically alter his fortunes, leading as it did to a contract with Warner Brothers studios.

His first screen credit was in the 1937 *Love Is On The Air*, while by just over two years later he had appeared in no less than nineteen Warner Brothers' movies.

President of the Screen Actors Guild for a time, his other screen credits included the 1940 *Santa Fe Trail*, *Hellcats of the Navy*, and *Bedtime for Bonzo*.

His final film was the 1964 *The Killers*, by which time his interest had focussed firmly on politics.

Formerly a Democrat, he had by now switched allegiance to the Republicans, and served as the Republican Governor of California from 1967 to 1975.

Sworn in as the 40th President of the United States of America in January of 1981, he survived an assassination attempt only three months later when he and his press secretary, a Secret Service agent, and a policeman were shot leaving a Washington hotel by John Hinckley.

Re-elected as president in a landslide victory in 1984, his second term of office is noted for successes such as the ending of the Cold War, but also for scandals that included the Iran-Contra affair.

Retiring from political life after his term as president ended in 1989, Reagan revealed five years later that he had been diagnosed with Alzheimer's disease.

He died in 2004, but his legacy lives on through a number of charities and foundations, including the Ronald Reagan Freedom Award – the highest civilian honour bestowed by the private Ronald Reagan Presidential Foundation.

Awarded to 'those who have made monumental and lasting contributions to the cause of freedom worldwide', past recipients of the honour include former Soviet President Mikhail Gorbachev, former British Prime Minister Margaret Thatcher, and former New York Mayor Rudy Giuliani.

Ronald Reagan had married the actress Jane Wyman in 1940, but the couple divorced eight years later.

In 1952 he married the actress Anne Francis Robbins, born in 1921 in Flushing, New York, and who became better known as First Lady of the United States **Nancy Reagan**.

Taking the stage name of Nancy Davis, she worked as an actress throughout the 1940s and 1950s, starring in films that included *Night into Morning* and *Hellcats of the Navy*, beside her future husband.

As First Lady she championed the cause of drug awareness and the 'Just Say No' anti-drug abuse campaign, while today she is actively involved in the promotion of stem-cell research.

Patti Davis, born Patricia Ann Reagan in Los Angeles in 1952, is the daughter of the former President and First Lady who lifestyle was often at odds with the conservative values of her parents.

This was controversially highlighted in 1994 when she posed for Playboy magazine.

A former actress who appeared in television shows that included *Love Boat* and *Fantasy Island*, she now pursues a career as a writer.

Her brother **Ron Reagan**, born in 1958 in Los Angeles, is a writer and political commentator and former talk show host, while her stepbrother **Michael Reagan** is a radio host.

Adopted by Ronald Reagan and his first wife Jane Wyman shortly after his birth in 1945, he at one time set world records for powerboat racing while raising money for a range of charities.

Born in 1941, **Maureen Reagan** was the daughter of the former President and Jane Wyman who, after a career as an actress, became an activist for the Republican Party.

At the time of her death in 2001 she was also a member of the board of directors of the Alzheimer's Association.

Christine, a second daughter of Ronald Reagan and Jane Wyman, died shortly after birth.

One of the most prominent members of President Reagan's political administration was **Donald Regan**, born in 1918 in Cambridge, Massachusetts, and who died in 2003.

The 66th United States Secretary of the Treasury from 1981 to 1985, he also served as Chief of Staff to the President from 1985 to 1987.

A distant ancestor of Ronald Reagan, **John Henninger Reagan** was the American politician born in 1818 in Sevier County, Tennessee.

Moving to Texas as a teenager and later becoming elected as a Democrat member of the House of Representatives, he left the House when Texas seceded from the Union and joined he Confederate States of America.

Serving in the cabinet of Jefferson Davis as Postmaster General during the Civil War of 1861 to 1865, he later became a founder of the Texas State Historical Association.

Reagan, who died in 1901, has been recognised as 'one of the four greatest Texans of the nineteenth century, along with Sam Houston, Stephen F. Austin, and James Stephen Hoggy.'

On the stage **Laura Regan**, born in 1977 in Halifax, Nova Scotia, is the Canadian actress whose film credits include the 2000 *Unbreakable*, the 2002 *They*, and the 2007 *Poor Boy's Game*.

She is also known for her role as Jessica Lynch in the television movie *Saving Jessica Lynch*, while she has also appeared in television shows that include *CSI: Miami*, and *Charmed*.

Her father is the former Nova Scotia Premier **Gerald Regan**, while her brother **Geoff Regan** is a former federal Minister of Fisheries and Oceans and her sister, **Nancy Regan**, host of Canada's *Live at Five's Nancy Regan*.

Also on the stage **Brian Regan** is the talented American stand-up comedian, renowned for his observational humour, who was born in 1965 in Miami.

Moving to New York in 1986, he won $10,000 two years later when he was named the 'Funniest Person in New York.'

Behind the camera lens **Denis O'Regan**, born in 1953 in London, is the rock music photographer who is recognised as having pioneered the use of auto focus cameras in the late 1980s and digital cameras in the late 1990s.

Bands he has toured with and photographed include Thin Lizzy, Pink Floyd, the Who, the Rolling Stones, and Duran Duran.

Also in the world of music **Tarik O'Regan**, born in 1978 in London, is the British composer of part North African roots whose compositions have been performed by, among others, the Los Angeles Master Chorale and the BBC Symphony Orchestra.

In the world of art **Michael Oman-Reagan** is the American artist born in 1976 in Columbia, Missouri, who specialises in placing art objects on, or near, buildings.

Born in 1936 in Washington, D.C., **Trudy Reagan** is the painter and founder of Ylem – an international organisation of artists, art curators, authors, and scientists.

Bearers of the Reagan name, in all its variety of spellings, have also excelled in the world of sport.

Born in Philadelphia in 1919, **Francis Reagan** was the talented American professional footballer who played for both the Philadelphia Eagles and the New York Giants in a career that lasted from 1941 to 1951.

The football safety died in 1972.

In baseball **William Regan**, born in 1899 in Pittsburgh, Pennsylvania, and who died in 1968, was the second baseman in Major League Baseball who played from 1926 to 1931 for teams that included the Boston Red Sox and the Pittsburgh Pirates.

As a player in the International League from 1931 until his retiral in 1935, he played for teams that included the Baltimore Orioles, Montreal Royals, and Toronto Maple Leafs.

Reagans and their namesakes can also make the rather unusual boast of having a number of fish species named in their honour – in particular in honour of **Charles Tate Regan**, the British ichthyologist who was born in 1878 in Sherbourne, Dorset, and who died in 1943.

Elected a fellow of the prestigious scientific 'think-tank' known as the Royal Society, he carried out extensive and meticulous work on fish classification schemes – and a number of species have been named regani in recognition of this.

Key dates in Ireland's history from the first settlers to the formation of the Irish Republic:

circa 7000 B.C.	Arrival and settlement of Stone Age people.
circa 3000 B.C.	Arrival of settlers of New Stone Age period.
circa 600 B.C.	First arrival of the Celts.
200 A.D.	Establishment of Hill of Tara, Co. Meath, as seat of the High Kings.
circa 432 A.D.	Christian mission of St. Patrick.
800-920 A.D.	Invasion and subsequent settlement of Vikings.
1002 A.D.	Brian Boru recognised as High King.
1014	Brian Boru killed at battle of Clontarf.
1169-1170	Cambro-Norman invasion of the island.
1171	Henry II claims Ireland for the English Crown.
1366	Statutes of Kilkenny ban marriage between native Irish and English.
1529-1536	England's Henry VIII embarks on religious Reformation.
1536	Earl of Kildare rebels against the Crown.
1541	Henry VIII declared King of Ireland.
1558	Accession to English throne of Elizabeth I.
1565	Battle of Affane.
1569-1573	First Desmond Rebellion.
1579-1583	Second Desmond Rebellion.
1594-1603	Nine Years War.
1606	Plantation' of Scottish and English settlers.
1607	Flight of the Earls.
1632-1636	Annals of the Four Masters compiled.
1641	Rebellion over policy of plantation and other grievances.
1649	Beginning of Cromwellian conquest.
1688	Flight into exile in France of Catholic Stuart monarch James II as Protestant Prince William of Orange invited to take throne of England along with his wife, Mary.
1689	William and Mary enthroned as joint monarchs; siege of Derry.
1690	Jacobite forces of James defeated by William at battle of the Boyne (July) and Dublin taken.

1691	Athlone taken by William; Jacobite defeats follow at Aughrim, Galway, and Limerick; conflict ends with Treaty of Limerick (October) and Irish officers allowed to leave for France.
1695	Penal laws introduced to restrict rights of Catholics; banishment of Catholic clergy.
1704	Laws introduced constricting rights of Catholics in landholding and public office.
1728	Franchise removed from Catholics.
1791	Foundation of United Irishmen republican movement.
1796	French invasion force lands in Bantry Bay.
1798	Defeat of Rising in Wexford and death of United Irishmen leaders Wolfe Tone and Lord Edward Fitzgerald.
1800	Act of Union between England and Ireland.
1803	Dublin Rising under Robert Emmet.
1829	Catholics allowed to sit in Parliament.
1845-1849	The Great Hunger: thousands starve to death as potato crop fails and thousands more emigrate.
1856	Phoenix Society founded.
1858	Irish Republican Brotherhood established.
1873	Foundation of Home Rule League.
1893	Foundation of Gaelic League.
1904	Foundation of Irish Reform Association.
1913	Dublin strikes and lockout.
1916	Easter Rising in Dublin and proclamation of an Irish Republic.
1917	Irish Parliament formed after Sinn Fein election victory.
1919-1921	War between Irish Republican Army and British Army.
1922	Irish Free State founded, while six northern counties remain part of United Kingdom as Northern Ireland, or Ulster; civil war up until 1923 between rival republican groups.
1949	Foundation of Irish Republic after all remaining constitutional links with Britain are severed.